Navigating the SRRV Visa Journey in the Philippines

Arthur Crandon LL.B (Hons.) M.A.

Navigating the SRRV Visa Journey in the Philippines

Copyright Arthur Crandon 2024

All rights reserved. No part of this book may be reproduced, stored in a retrieval system, or transmitted in any form or by any means—electronic, mechanical, photocopying, recording, or otherwise—without the prior written permission of the publisher, except for brief quotations in critical reviews or articles.

This is a work of fiction. Names, characters, places, and incidents are either the product of the author's imagination or used fictitiously. Any resemblance to actual persons, living or dead, events, or locales is entirely coincidental.

ISBN: 9798342090902
Cover design by Lynnie Ceniza
Interior design and formatting by Lynnie Ceniza
Published by Arthur Crandon Publishing
Visit our website: Arthurcrandon.co.uk

DISCLAIMER

The information provided in this book is for general informational purposes only. It does not constitute legal, financial, or professional advice. While every effort has been made to ensure accuracy, the author and publisher assume no responsibility for errors or omissions. Readers should consult with appropriate professionals for specific advice tailored to their individual circumstances.

First Edition: August 2024

The SRRV Visa is the most expensive of the Visas on offer from the Philippine Government, with a high initial fee and a high annual fee. But, there is no doubt that the benefits it provides surpasses any other visa arrangement

CONTENTS

	Acknowledgments	i
1	Summary	1
2	The Benefits of an SRRV	9
3	Can I work with an SRRV Visa?	13
4	Are there any restrictions?	17
5	Foreign Investments	21
6	Tax	25
7	Real Estate	29

If you are considering retiring to the Philippines. There are many isa options available to you. There are more if you are married to a local. Take your time before you decide.

1 SUMMARY

The **Special Resident Retiree's Visa (SRRV)** is a special non-immigrant visa designed for foreign nationals who wish to make the Philippines their second home or retirement destination. Here are the key details:

1. **Purpose**: The SRRV allows retirees to live in the Philippines indefinitely and enjoy multiple-entry privileges. It's an excellent option for those seeking a peaceful retirement or investment opportunities in this beautiful country.

2. **Eligibility and Benefits**:

! The Special Resident Retiree's Visa (SRRV) in the Philippines is an excellent option for retirees looking to settle in this beautiful country. Let's dive into the requirements:

1. **Eligibility Criteria**:

   - You must be at least **50 years old** if you're a foreign national. However, if you're a non-residential Filipino, the age requirement is **35 years and above**.

   - Alternatively, you can qualify by making a deposit:

     - **With Pension**: Deposit **$10,000** and maintain a monthly pension of at least **$800** (for single applicants).

     - **Without Pension**: Make a deposit of at least **$50,000**.

2. **Basic Requirements**:

   - **Application Form**: Complete the SRRV application form.

   - **Valid Passport**: Ensure your passport has a valid Philippine Tourist Visa.

- **Medical Clearance**: Obtain a medical certificate from any licensed physician in the Philippines.

- **National Bureau of Investigation (NBI) Clearance** or police clearance from your country of origin.

- **Photos (2x2)**: You'll need eight passport-sized photos.

- **Original Passport Details**: Note down your passport number, entry date, and expiry date.

- **Bank Certification**: Provide proof of funds by showing a bank certification.

3. **Additional Requirements** (Depending on Your Situation):

    - **Proof of Relationship**: If applicable, submit marriage certificates, birth certificates, or household registers.

    - **Classic with Pension**: Former Filipino (Age > 35 years): PSA Birth Certificate or old Philippine

Passport.

- Retired Diplomat (Age > 50 years): Certificate of Employment.

- Expanded Courtesy (Age > 50 years): Certificate from the concerned agency.

- **Human Touch**:

    - Medical Certificate for Pre-Existing Medical Condition.

    - Proof of Pension (at least $1,500).

    - Health Insurance Coverage (acceptable in the Philippines).

    - If you had a previous visa (e.g., 9G, 13A, 47A2), provide the order of issuance or downgrading.

- **Waiver of Liability**: Required for some cases.

4.

5. **Fees**:
   - **Processing/Service Fee**: $1,400 (for all applicants).

   - **Annual PRA Fee**: $360 (per year).

   - **ID Fee** (for SRRV Courtesy only): $10 per applicant per year.

Remember that additional supporting documents may be requested during the pre-evaluation process, and the processing of your SRRV application will begin once you've submitted all necessary documents and paid the required fees. If your tourist visa expires during the process, you'll need to cover the extension cost.

- **Multiple Entry Privileges**: SRRV holders can enter and exit the Philippines as often as they like without needing additional visas.

- **Work, Study, and Investment**: SRRV holders are eligible to work, study, and invest in the Philippines.

- **Discounts and Perks**: SRRV holders enjoy discounts from PRA-accredited partners, a free subscription to the PRA Newsletter, and assistance with government agency transactions.

- **Access to PhilHealth**: SRRV holders can avail themselves of PhilHealth benefits and privileges.

3. **Types of SRRV**:

    - **SRRV Classic**: For active and healthy retirees. The visa deposit varies based on pension status:
        - Applicants aged 50 and above without a pension: US$20,000
        - Applicants aged 50 and above with a pension: US$10,000 (monthly pension of US$800 for single applicants or US$1,000 for applicants with dependents)

    - **SRRV Courtesy**: For former Filipinos (50 years old and above) and foreign nationals (50 years old and above) who have served in the Philippines as ambassadors or diplomats. The visa deposit is US$1,500. This program was expanded to include other groups, such as honorary consuls and retirees of international organizations.

4. **Application Process**:

    o   Accomplish the SRRV Application Form.

    o   Obtain an original Medical Certificate from a licensed physician or accredited clinic in the Philippines.

    o   Secure a Police Clearance from your country of origin or last residence abroad (translated to English and authenticated).

    o   Submit the necessary documents and fees to the Philippine Retirement Authority (PRA).

Remember that the SRRV is a lifetime visa, granting you the opportunity to enjoy the Philippines' warm hospitality, stunning landscapes, and vibrant culture. If you're considering it, I recommend reaching out to the PRA for the most up-to-date information and personalized guidance.

2 THE BENEFITS OF AN SRRV

The **Special Resident Retiree's Visa (SRRV)** is a unique offering by the Philippine government, tailor-made for those considering the Philippines as their retirement haven or a place to invest. Let's dive into the advantages that make the SRRV an appealing choice:

1. **Permanent Residency**: Unlike some other retirement visas, the SRRV grants you permanent residency status. No more visa renewals or worrying about overstaying your welcome—this is your second home.

2. **Indefinite Stay**: Picture this: you can enjoy an extended or permanent retirement in the Philippines. The SRRV allows you to stay indefinitely, which means you can explore the country's splendid beaches,

captivating landscapes, and warm hospitality without time constraints.

3. **Multiple Entry Privileges**: With the SRRV, you have the flexibility to travel in and out of the Philippines without hassle. Say goodbye to restrictive visa renewals and hello to seamless trips.

4. **Exemption from Certain Taxes**: Retirees holding an SRRV enjoy tax benefits. Foreign pension and annuities? Exempt. It's like a financial sigh of relief.

5. **Import Duty Exemption**: When you move to the Philippines, you can bring along your personal effects and household goods duty-free. Up to $7,000 USD worth of stuff—now that's a smooth transition.

6. **Travel Tax Exemption**: Traveling becomes more affordable. As an SRRV holder, you're exempt from the travel tax. More savings for your adventures!

7. **Investment Opportunities**: Want to invest in the Philippines? The SRRV opens doors for you. Whether it's property or business ventures, you're in the game.

8. **Simplified Business Registration**: If you're eyeing business opportunities, the SRRV simplifies the registration process. Less bureaucracy, more entrepreneurship.

Remember, like any good thing, there are considerations. Financial requirements exist, and paperwork is part of the deal. But for many retirees, the SRRV Visa offers a delightful blend of tropical paradise and modern living—a chance to call the Philippines home

3 CAN I WORK WITH AN SRRV VISA?

1. **Can You Work with an SRRV?**

    o **Short Answer**: No, the SRRV alone does not grant you work privileges in the Philippines.

    o **Separate Work Permit**: If you want to work, you'll need to apply for an Alien Employment Permit (AEP) separately. The SRRV doesn't automatically cover employment rights.

If you're considering working in the Philippines, you'll need to navigate the visa process. Let's dive into the essentials:

1. **Types of Work Visas**:

    - **9 (g) Pre-Arranged Employee Commercial Visa**: This visa is for foreign nationals who have secured employment with a Philippine-based company. It's suitable for those working in various industries.

    - **9 (g) Pre-Arranged Employee Non-Commercial Visa**: Similar to the commercial visa, but for non-commercial purposes (e.g., missionaries, volunteers, etc.).

    - **Special Non-Immigrant Visa (47 (A) (2))**: This visa is specific to regional operating headquarters (ROHQs) and is governed by Executive Order 226, as amended by Republic Act 8756.

    - **Work Permits**:

        - **Special Work Permit (SWP)**: For short-term work assignments (usually up to six months).

- **Provisional Work Permit (PWP)**: Temporary permit while awaiting the Alien Employment Permit (AEP).

- **Alien Employment Permit (AEP)**: Essential for long-term employment.

2. **Requirements for a Work Visa**:

   - **Completed 9 (g) Work Visa Application Form**: Obtain this form and fill it out.

   - **Valid Passport**: Ensure your passport is up-to-date.

   - **Notarized Certification of Employer's Number of Foreign and Filipino Employees**: Your employer will provide this.

   - **Certified Copy of Alien Employment Permit (AEP)**: The Department of Labor and Employment (DOLE) issues this permit.

- **Certificate of Clearance from the Philippines Bureau of Immigration (B.I.)**: This clearance confirms that you're eligible to work in the country.

Remember, the process can vary based on your specific circumstances, so it's advisable to consult with legal experts or the Philippine Bureau of Immigration for personalized guidance.

4 ARE THERE ANY RESTRICTIONS?

If you're considering working in the Philippines, you'll need to navigate the visa process. Let's dive into the essentials:

1. **Types of Work Visas**:

    - **9 (g) Pre-Arranged Employee Commercial Visa**: This visa is for foreign nationals who have secured employment with a Philippine-based company. It's suitable for those working in various industries.

    - **9 (g) Pre-Arranged Employee Non-Commercial Visa**: Similar to the commercial visa, but for non-commercial purposes (e.g., missionaries, volunteers, etc.).

- **Special Non-Immigrant Visa (47 (A) (2))**: This visa is specific to regional operating headquarters (ROHQs) and is governed by Executive Order 226, as amended by Republic Act 8756.

- **Work Permits**:

    - **Special Work Permit (SWP)**: For short-term work assignments (usually up to six months).

    - **Provisional Work Permit (PWP)**: Temporary permit while awaiting the Alien Employment Permit (AEP).

    - **Alien Employment Permit (AEP)**: Essential for long-term employment.

2. **Requirements for a Work Visa**:

    - **Completed 9 (g) Work Visa Application Form**: Obtain this form and fill it out.

- **Valid Passport**: Ensure your passport is up-to-date.

- **Notarized Certification of Employer's Number of Foreign and Filipino Employees**: Your employer will provide this.

- **Certified Copy of Alien Employment Permit (AEP)**: The Department of Labor and Employment (DOLE) issues this permit.

- **Certificate of Clearance from the Philippines Bureau of Immigration (B.I.)**: This clearance confirms that you're eligible to work in the country.

Remember, the process can vary based on your specific circumstances, so it's advisable to consult with legal experts or the Philippine Bureau of Immigration for personalized guidance.

5 FOREIGN INVESTMENT

Ah, foreign investment—the lifeblood of economic growth and cross-cultural exchange! Let's dive into the Philippines, shall we?

Foreign Investment in the Philippines: A Quick Overview

The Philippines has been doing a little regulatory cha-cha with foreign investment over the years. Here's the lowdown:

1. **Foreign Investment Act (FIA)**: The FIA, enacted in 1991, is the main player here. It's like the backstage pass for foreign

investors. The act has actually been quite the liberalizer, opening the doors (or perhaps the bamboo gates) to foreign capital and technology.

2. **No Restrictions on Export Enterprises**: If you're thinking of setting up an export-oriented business in the Philippines, you're in luck! There are generally no restrictions on how much foreign ownership you can have in these enterprises. So, if you want to export the world's finest mangoes or create a line of bespoke jeepneys for global consumption, go ahead!

3. **Domestic Market Enterprises**: Now, when it comes to enterprises serving mainly the domestic market, the vibe changes a bit. Foreign investments are welcome, but they're meant to play second fiddle to Filipino capital and tech. It's like a friendly duet: "You take the high notes, we'll handle the harmonies."

4. **Recent Changes**: The Philippines has been jazzing things up lately. Amendments to the Public Services Act (PSA) have flung open previously closed sectors to 100 percent foreign investment. Imagine the PSA as the grand ballroom where foreign

investors can now waltz freely with local partners

5. **COVID-19 and Other Hurdles**: Of course, no dance is without its challenges. Investment promotion agencies (IPAs) have pointed out that the pandemic, high business costs, and lingering equity restrictions can sometimes trip up foreign investors. But hey, every tango needs a few dramatic dips, right?
6.
7. **Record FDI Inflows**: Despite the occasional misstep, the Philippines has been catching some investment waves. In 2021, foreign direct investment (FDI) inflows did the limbo—bending backward to a record USD 10.5 billion.

6 TAX

Taxation for foreign investors can be a bit of a maze, but let's navigate it together.

When Americans invest in stocks or bonds from companies based overseas, there's a double whammy: Uncle Sam wants a slice of the pie, and the home country of that foreign firm might also come knocking for its share. It's like a global potluck where everyone brings their tax appetites.
Here's the scoop:

1. **U.S. Income Tax**: When you, as an American investor, earn money from foreign investments (like dividends or

capital gains), the U.S. government wants its cut. Yep, even if those profits are coming from a Swiss chocolate company or an Australian kangaroo farm.

2. **Foreign Taxes**: Now, the twist—many countries have their own tax rules. Some are chill (no capital gains tax, anyone?), while others are a bit more assertive. For instance:

    o   Italy does a 26% cha-cha with non-residents selling Italian stocks.

    o   Spain does a 19% flamenco on gains from Spanish stocks.

3. **The Foreign Tax Credit**: Fear not! The U.S. tax code has a secret handshake: the "foreign tax credit." It's like saying, "Hey, Uncle Sam, I already paid taxes elsewhere. Cut me some slack!"

    o   If you've paid foreign taxes (on income, dividends, or interest), you can claim either a tax credit or a deduction on your U.S. tax return.

    o   Opt for the credit—it's like a direct discount on your tax bill. A $200 credit means $200 less to Uncle Sam.

- The deduction is simpler math but less exciting. If you're in the 25% tax bracket, a $200 deduction only shaves $50 off your bill.

4. **Paper Trail**: Keep an eye out for those IRS love letters (okay, maybe not love, but still). If you hold foreign investments, you'll get a 1099-DIV or 1099-INT at year's end. These forms reveal how much foreign tax was withheld from your earnings.

Remember, every country dances to its own tax tune. So, before you waltz into international investments, do a little tax tango—research local rates and understand the rules

7 REAL ESTATE

The allure of foreign real estate! Whether it's a cozy cottage in the Tuscan hills, a beachfront condo in Bali, or a charming chalet nestled in the Swiss Alps, there's something magical about owning property in another corner of the world.

Now, let's dive into the tax waters, shall we? Here's the scoop on the tax implications of investing in real estate abroad:

1. **Similarities to U.S. Property Tax Treatment**:

    - The tax treatment of homes is surprisingly similar whether they're perched on American soil or tucked away in a foreign land. You can still enjoy some familiar perks:

- **Mortgage Interest Deduction**: Just like back home, you can deduct mortgage interest and mortgage points on your foreign property. The limit is $750,000 of secured mortgage debt (or $375,000 if you're married and filing separately). Remember, though, this requires itemizing on your tax return.

- **Personal Use Property**: If you use the property as a second home (not for rental), you can deduct mortgage interest and discount points as you would for a second home in the U.S.

- **Previous Property Purchases**: If you bought your properties before December 16, 2017, you get the previous deduction limit of $1 million in qualified mortgage debt. (Ah, the good ol' days!)

- **Home Office Deduction**: But hold your horses—expenses like utilities, maintenance, and insurance aren't deductible unless you qualify for the elusive home office deduction.

2. **Rental Income and Expenses**:

    o Now, let's say you're channeling your inner landlord and renting out that overseas abode. Here's the lowdown:

        - **Rental Income**: If you're raking in rental income, the tax rules depend on how many days you use the home for personal bliss versus rental business. Keep meticulous records!

        - **Deductible Expenses**: You can deduct "ordinary and necessary expenses for managing, conserving, and maintaining" the property. Think mortgage interest, property insurance, repairs, and even those jaunts to check on your place.

- **Foreign Property Taxes**: Brace yourself—unlike mortgage interest, foreign property taxes are no longer deductible on your U.S. tax return. That deduction sailed away in 2017.

3. **Capital Gains and Selling Abroad**:

    - When you eventually sell that charming chalet (or the beachfront condo where you perfected your piña colada recipe), you'll face capital gains tax. This applies whether you're in the Rockies or the Maldives.

    - **Reporting Requirements**: Selling foreign property means reporting capital gains or losses on your U.S. tax return. Uncle Sam wants to know!

    - **Local Taxes**: Remember, you'll also be paying property and capital gains taxes in the country where your slice of paradise resides.

4. **Country-Specific Nuances**:

    o Every country dances to its own tax tune. So, before you waltz into foreign real estate, learn the local steps. Seek advice from tax experts who specialize in international matters. They're like the travel guides of the tax world.

In summary, investing in real estate abroad isn't just about sunsets and sea views—it's about understanding the tax tides. So, whether you're sipping espresso in Rome or samba-ing in Rio, keep those receipts handy and consult a tax pro

ABOUT THE AUTHOR

Arthur Crandon is a retired lawyer and a prolific writer. He is British and grew up in a rural community in Somerset. He has lived in England, Wales, Hong Kong and the Philippines and now spends most of his time in the Philippines with his Visayan wife and their son.

He loves to hear from anyone who has anything to do with the Philippines – you can email him anytime on:

ac@arthurcrandon.co.uk

www.ingramcontent.com/pod-product-compliance
Lightning Source LLC
Chambersburg PA
CBHW070950220526
45471CB00007B/2971